Little Bunny peeked outside.
There was Fox, sitting in the grass.

"Will I ever get those carrots?" said Little Bunny.
"I bet I never will!"

Mother Rabbit just laughed.
"Never say never," she said.

Little Bunny had an idea.
He covered himself with grass.

Little Bunny almost got to the carrots.
Then Fox said, "Why is that grass moving?
Is that YOU, Little Bunny?"

Little Bunny ran back home.

"Will I ever get those carrots?" he said.

"I bet I never will!"

Mother Rabbit just laughed.
Then she helped Little Bunny take off the grass.
"Never say never," she said.

Little Bunny had another idea.
He took a rope and made a loop.

Little Bunny almost got the carrots with the rope.
Then Fox said, "What is that rope doing there?
Is that YOU again, Little Bunny?"

Little Bunny ran back home.

"Will I ever get those carrots?" he said.

"I bet I never will!"

Mother Rabbit just laughed.
Then she helped Little Bunny put the rope away.
"Never say never," she said.

Little Bunny peeked outside.
There was Fox, sitting in the grass.
But he was asleep!

14

So, very quietly, Little Bunny just hopped
through the grass and got those carrots.

Little Bunny ran back home.
"You see, Little Bunny," his mother said,
"I told you never to say never!"
And they both laughed.